Titanic

Matt Ralphs

Illustrated by
Elena Dall'Aglio

Collins

Stern
Boat Deck
Aft Well Deck
Main Engine Room
Poop Deck
Steering Gear Room
P
O
N
M
L
K
J
Rudder
Electricity Room
Boiler Rooms 1 to 6

Port
Lifeboats
Boat Deck
Second-Class entrance
Lifeboats
Starboard

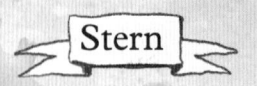

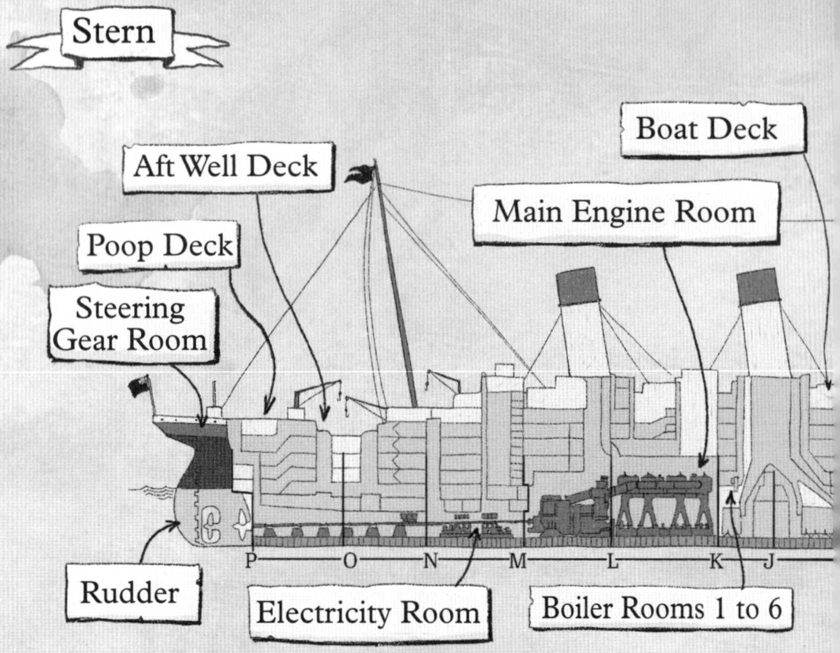

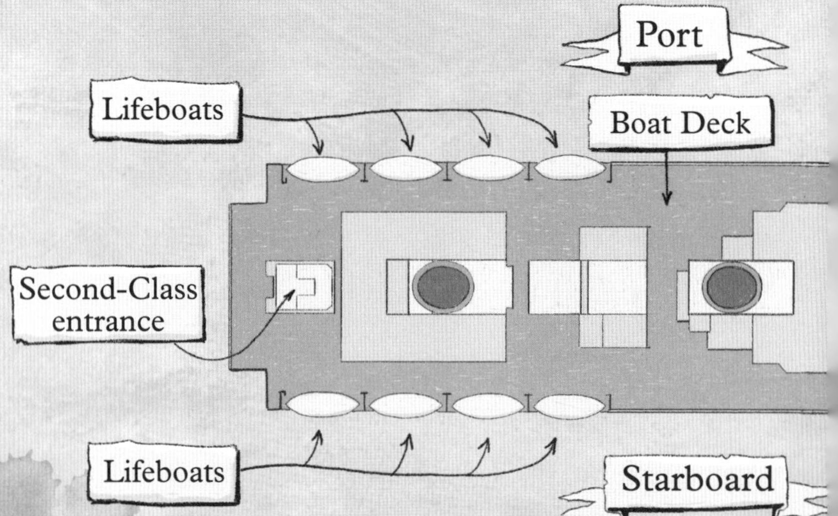

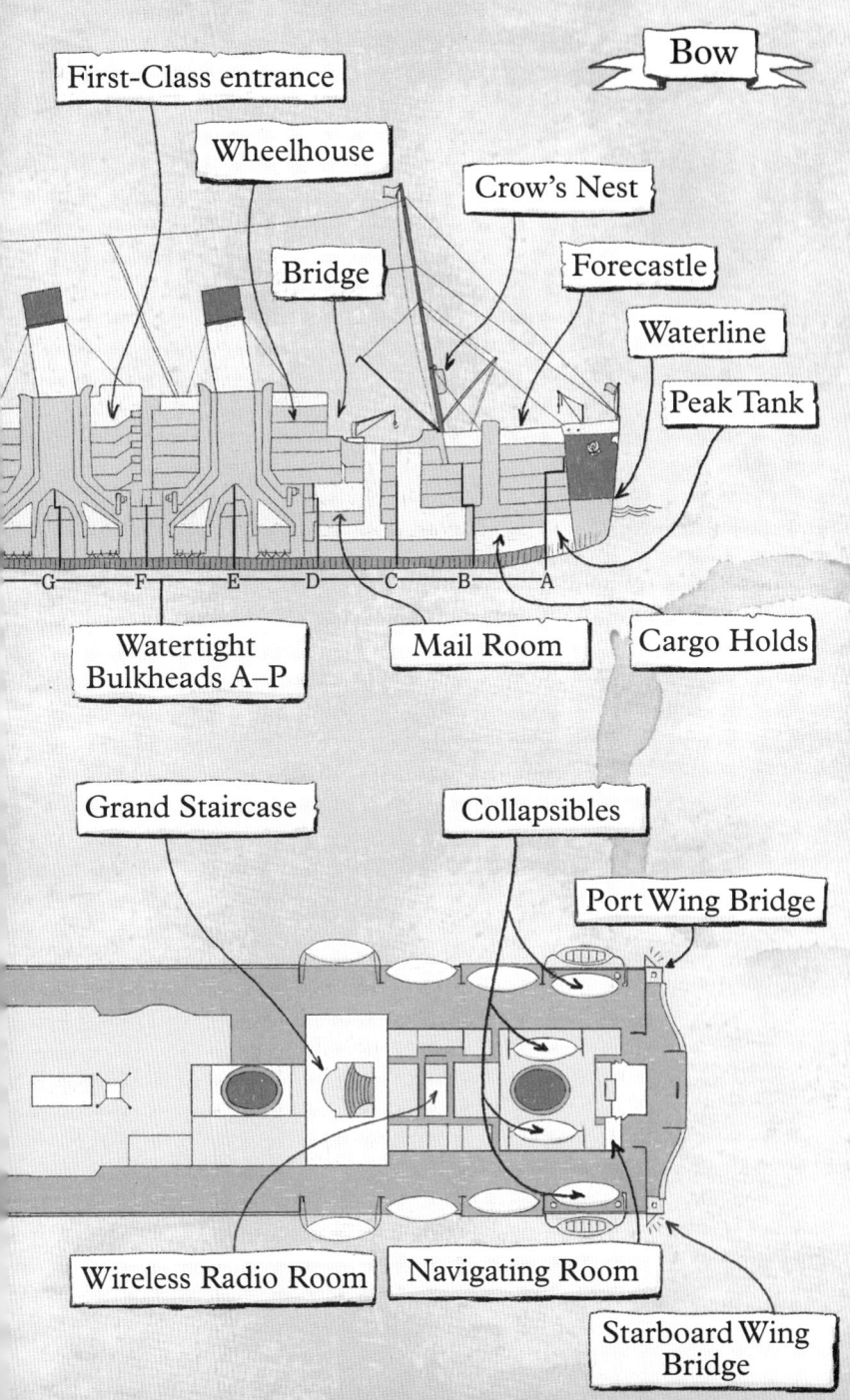

14th April, 1912, 11:30 p.m.

RMS *Titanic* cuts through the sea like a knife through satin. Her front three funnels, tall and elegant, pour black smoke into the night sky. At the rear, a trio of bronze propellers churns the water to froth. From blade-like bow to rounded stern, this magnificent ship – the largest moving human-made object in the world – blazes with light.

The North Atlantic can be a dangerous place even for a ship as big as this one. But not tonight.

Tonight, the sea is calm enough for *Titanic* to cast a reflection – a shimmering sister ship gliding beneath the water.

The only downside was the sudden drop in temperature that began just after sunset, forcing most passengers to retreat to the heated public areas or the comfort of their beds. However, a few hardy souls still brave the cold to stroll the open decks, not quite ready to end what has been a relaxing and enjoyable day.

Meanwhile, in the kitchens, bakeries, pantries, laundries, storerooms, workshops, offices and many other places on this vast and maze-like ship, the crew work ceaselessly to ensure everything runs like oiled clockwork.

Titanic is five days into her **maiden voyage** from Southampton to New York and carries 1,317 passengers and 891 crew. The Atlantic's water temperature is just below freezing. The closest land is 640 kilometres away. The seabed is four kilometres down.

All is well.

11:39 p.m.

Lookouts Frederick Fleet and Reginald Lee have been on watch up in the crow's nest for nearly two hours. With a clear view ahead, they are the ship's eyes and first warning of trouble. Their breath fogs, their noses run, and their fingers stay numb no matter how much they blow on them, but these professional sailors don't for a second take their eyes off the sea.

They've been ordered to keep a sharp lookout for icebergs, and in this vital duty, they are vigilant and watchful ... but not especially worried. After all, the night is clear, and both men are confident they'll spot ice early enough to allow *Titanic* plenty of time to avoid it. And yet, despite the clear air, Fleet notices something unusual: the dazzling canopy of stars above isn't quite reaching down to the horizon. It's as if the lowest stars are obscured by a dark haze.

Before he can mention this to Lee, Fleet sees something *far* more disturbing – a black mass, dead ahead, emerging from the haze and getting rapidly larger.

Quickly realising what he's seeing, and how frighteningly close it is, Fleet rings the brass warning bell three times and picks up the telephone connecting the crow's nest to the bridge.

"Is anybody there?" Fleet says.

"Yes," a voice crackles. "What did you see?"

"Iceberg, right ahead!"

"Thank you."

The line goes dead.

First Officer William Murdoch is *Titanic*'s third most senior crew member. He began his shift as Officer of the Watch at 10:00 p.m., which means the responsibility of navigating the ship and ensuring the safety of every soul on board is his until 2:00 a.m.

Tonight, he is taking no chances. He knows there's ice about because *Titanic*'s wireless operators received several warnings that day from other ships in the area.

Wrapped in a thick overcoat and staring ahead from under the brim of his officer's cap, Murdoch stands watch on the starboard wing bridge – an open area to the right of the main bridge.

His eyes are well adjusted to the dark. He sees quite clearly the white cargo crane and canvas hatch covers on the forward well deck below, and the crow's nest, above and to his left. Beyond the forecastle railing, the sea is a black mirror filled with stars.

Murdoch sees the iceberg a second before Fleet rings the warning bell. A dark bulk emerging from a dark haze. After taking a moment to judge its size, and the distance to the iceberg, he dashes to the bridge. Murdoch arrives just as Sixth Officer James Moody finishes his telephone conversation with Fleet.

"Iceberg, right ahead!" Moody reports.

"Hard-a-starboard!" Murdoch yells, and yanks the **engine telegraph** handle from the FULL AHEAD position to STOP. He crosses the bridge and does the same to the port engine telegraph. These actions will instruct Chief Engineer Joseph Bell, located way down in the main engine room, to stop *Titanic*'s engines.

Meanwhile, in the wheelhouse at the back of the bridge – and under the watchful eye of Sixth Officer Moody – Quartermaster Robert Hichens obeys Murdoch's order and spins the ship's wheel counterclockwise as quickly as he can.

Inside the steering gear room, located on C-Deck, right at the very back of the ship, a black-and-cream painted steam engine responds to Hichen's wheel-turn. It clanks into motion: gears shift, valves hiss, cogged wheels mesh and rotate. Outside, connected to the steam engine by a huge steel shaft, *Titanic*'s seven-storey high, 91-tonne rudder begins to move.

Chief Engineer Joseph Bell stands in the middle of *Titanic*'s main engine room, tea mug in hand, proudly surveying his mechanical domain. Located directly beneath the rearmost funnel, this cavernous space spreads the whole width of the ship, and rises from the lowest deck – the Tank Top – all the way to D-Deck. It contains the two biggest **reciprocating steam engines** ever built. Each one is three storeys tall and weighs 653 tonnes.

The steel walls echo with their labours: the press-and-hiss of plunging pistons, the clank-and-churn of the connecting rods, the steady rumble of the connecting rods turning the ship's propellers. Bell's engineers add to the noise, calling to each other from a network of ladders, platforms and catwalks.

During the day, natural light pours down from a skylight high above on the Boat Deck, but at this late hour, the whole place is lit by electric bulbs. Shadows are deep, and the air so thick with oil and grease you almost have to wade through it.

"They're running well," Bell says to a nearby colleague. "We'll get to New York early at this rate."

The conversation is cut short. A warning bell chimes from the main engine room telegraph and a pointer moves automatically to the STOP position – this is Murdoch's order coming through from up on the bridge.

Decades of crossing the world's oceans in thundering engine rooms has taught Bell that orders must be delivered swiftly and clearly.

"Stop engines!" he bellows.

Bell's voice carries over the din, driving his men into action: spinning control wheels, closing valves and starving the engines of the steam they need to function. Satisfied with the speed and discipline of his engineers, but concerned about this sudden and unexpected turn of events, Bell pulls the telegraph handle to the STOP position to inform Murdoch that his order has been received and carried out.

Below the waterline, the three enormous propellers begin to slow down. It will take around 30 seconds for them to stop completely, after which *Titanic* will go into an unpowered drift.

"Is the wheel hard-over, Mr Hichens?" Murdoch calls from the bridge.

"Aye, sir! Hard-over," says Hichens, confirming the wheel is as far as it can go.

Quartermaster Hichens doesn't like the tension in the normally calm First Officer's voice.

He also doesn't like not being able to see what's happening outside. The wheelhouse has five windows looking into the bridge, but at night their blinds are drawn. This is to prevent the light given off by the wheelhouse compass from shining into the bridge and ruining the men's night-vision. All Hichens can do is keep the wheel hard-over, place his trust in the officers, and hope for the best.

Murdoch, on the other hand, sees *exactly* what's happening.

Titanic is speeding directly towards a glistening mountain of ice. It's shaped like a fang – wide at the waterline and tapering to a point – and Murdoch can tell it's at least the height of the Boat Deck. He also knows that the bulk of the ice, amounting to millions of granite-hard tonnes, is hidden beneath the sea.

Sweat trickles down his back as he wills the ship to turn.

11:40 p.m.

Fleet grips the edge of the crow's nest rail as the blue-white iceberg and its perfect reflection grows, widens and swells until it seems to fill his entire field of view.

"Come on," he mutters. "*Turn*, can't you?"

Titanic, as the name suggests, is enormous. She has ten decks, weighs over 47,000 tonnes, stretches 269 metres, and towers 53 metres from top to bottom. And yet, despite her size, she's agile, and it takes only 37 seconds from Hichens' wheel-turn for the great ship to start swinging to port.

To Fleet, the iceberg appears to drift ... with agonising slowness ... rightward. As the central peak slides away from *Titanic*'s bow and towards her starboard side, he begins to hope that disaster's been avoided by the barest of margins.

Beneath the water, *Titanic* strikes a **spur** of ice jutting from the berg. As she passes, the spur rubs along her starboard side, scraping paint and punching six narrow splits of varying lengths between her steel hull plates. The damaged areas stretch from the Peak Tank all the way back to Number 5 Boiler Room.

The impact lasts six seconds.

Murdoch feels a vibration as *Titanic*'s bow swings into the clear. A teacup left on the chart table rattles in its saucer. Ice chunks knocked loose by the impact shatter and slide all over the well deck below. For a moment, the iceberg fills the side window, then it's gone.

Wanting to push the stern away from the iceberg to avoid further damage, Murdoch bellows "Hard-a-port!" to Hichens.

"Hard-a-port! Aye, sir!" The white-faced Quartermaster spins the wheel clockwise.

Certain the ship is damaged (although unaware how badly) Murdoch turns the switch to close her watertight doors.

John Jacob Astor, the richest passenger on the ship and returning from his honeymoon in Europe, is one of the few hardy souls taking a stroll outside on the Boat Deck. He's gazing up at the stars when he feels a faint grinding sensation. A few seconds later, something white and triangular glides silently past the ship.

"Was that a sail?" he mutters.

One deck below, a gaggle of excited passengers and white uniformed **stewards** burst outside from the First-Class lounge to see what has jolted the ship.

From the back of the ship, a voice cries, "An iceberg has passed us."

In one of the luxurious First-Class passenger suites on C-Deck, John Jacob Astor's pregnant wife, Madeleine, sits at her dressing table writing a letter. A judder – strong enough to form ripples in her water glass – inspires an image in her mind of a giant finger rubbing along the ship.

Stewards laying tables in the huge Second-Class dining saloon on D-Deck look up as a vibration heavy enough to rattle the silverware shivers under their feet.

Further down on G-Deck, in a plain but spotless dormitory near the bow, the lamp trimmer Samuel Hemming (whose job is to look after the ship's many oil lamps) is woken by what sounds like a roll of thunder and a jolt strong enough to shake his bunk. As his crewmates grumble and groan, he quickly dresses and heads up to see what's going on.

Located nine metres below the waterline, *Titanic*'s six boiler rooms are the red-hot guts of the ship. They contain 29 towering boilers that burn coal, boil water and pipe high-pressure steam to the main engine room. These giant kettles consume around 550 tonnes of coal per day, and every shovelful is fed into their blazing furnaces by hand. For *Titanic*'s 180 firemen, it's backbreaking, sweltering – but well-paid – work.

Leading Fireman Fred Barrett watches his sweat-and-dirt-streaked gang of eight firemen from the starboard side of Number 6 Boiler Room. Not much can be heard over the crunch of shovels digging into coal piles, the scrape as it's hurled into the furnaces, and the roar as it burns. Orange firelight bathes the steel walls and stairways. The air shimmers. Smoke swirls.

Barrett tenses as a warning bell rings and the Boiler Room's telegraph lights up STOP. This order – repeated in the other five boiler rooms – means the ship is stopping, and the boilers must be dampened down to reduce the amount of steam rushing towards the main engine room.

"Shut all **dampers**!" he shouts.

His men jump to it, dropping their shovels and slamming the furnace doors.

Before Barrett has a chance to wonder why the ship is stopping, there comes a screech of tortured metal. The hull plates right behind where he's standing bulge inward and split. Pipes snap, girders buckle, and the starboard-most boiler shifts on its foundations. That's all Barrett sees before he's shoved halfway across the room by a torrent of ice-cold seawater.

The chaos is sudden and terrifying. Men cry out as the sea rages around them; some swarm up the escape ladders; others, including Barrett, scramble under the lowering watertight door into Number 5 Boiler Room.

It's stunned silence on the bridge. The iceberg has gone, and the dread-inducing shudder has stopped. It's almost as if nothing has happened. Murdoch slowly lets out the breath he's been holding.

"What have we struck?"

This calm voice belongs to Captain Edward Smith, *Titanic*'s commander and the most experienced officer in the White Star Line, the shipping company who own her. He'd been working in his cabin when he felt the vibration.

"An iceberg, sir," Murdoch replies. "I turned the ship to starboard and stopped the engines. I then turned to port, but she hit before I could do anymore."

"Close the watertight doors."

"I've already done so, sir."

Smith leads Murdoch onto the starboard wing bridge, and they peer down the length of the ship. Fourth Officer Joseph Boxhall emerges from the officer's quarters and joins them after being alerted by the impact.

"No sign of the iceberg now," Murdoch says.

Smith turns to Boxhall. "Go down and find the carpenter. Tell him to assess the damage and report back to me. And see if you can find Mr Andrews as well."

Boxhall nods and hurries off. Smith and Murdoch exchange an anxious glance and head back to the bridge.

Below, on the well deck, a few Third-Class passengers laugh and cheer as they kick around the lumps of ice.

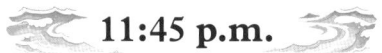
11:45 p.m.

When lamp trimmer Samuel Hemming emerges onto the well deck and sees ice scattered over the polished pine boards, he realises it was an iceberg impact that woke him. Curious, he climbs the "crew only" ladder onto the forecastle and leans over the starboard railing to see if there's any damage. Nothing visible from this angle, but Hemming does notice how small *Titanic*'s bow wave is.

She's slowing down, he thinks.

Then he notices something else – a hissing sound coming from further forward. After passing the massive anchor chains, he reaches the lowered deck section that houses the 14-tonne central anchor. Hemming is now as far forward as it's possible to go.

The sound, more of a gasp than a hiss, comes from a vent pipe. This pipe is an opening in the hull just below the railing. It goes right down into the Peak Tank, *Titanic*'s deepest and forward-most compartment. Hemming knows this gasp is the sound of floodwater forcing air out of the Peak Tank.

After listening for a minute or two, he wanders back towards the well deck. Clearly *Titanic* is taking on water, and quickly by the sounds of it, but if the flooding is limited to the Peak Tank she'll easily stay afloat. Unconcerned, he leans on the railing to watch Third-Class passengers throw ice up into B-Deck for some curious Second-Class passengers to examine.

That's when he notices the canvas sheets covering the well deck cargo hatches billowing upwards, as if air's being forced out by floodwater there too.

The impact disturbed a fair number of people, especially those housed forward like the off-duty firemen and stewards resting in their dormitories, and Second- and Third-Class passengers asleep in their cabins.

However, far more people are roused by the silence following the shutdown of the engines. After four days at sea, everyone is used to their constant throb, as well as the many other ways by which they make themselves known: the slight vibration beneath the feet, the creak of wooden fittings, the *chink* of glassware knocking together, the slice-and-wash of the foaming bow wave.

All this noise and sensation ... gone.

It's unnerving.

Passengers all over the ship emerge from their beds, poke their heads out into the corridors and ask passing crew what's happened. But the crew don't know what's going on either, so they just reply, "Nothing to worry about," and go about their business.

Violet Jessop is lying in bed wondering what on earth that terrible crunching and ripping sound had been when a fellow **stewardess** knocks on her cabin door and looks in.

"Get dressed, Violet," she says. "And put on a lifejacket."

"Why? What has happened?"

"We've struck something and are taking on water."

Violet jumps out of bed and gathers her clothes. "How bad is it?"

"I don't know. Best head up to the Boat Deck and see what you can do."

It takes Violet less than four minutes to put on her uniform and lifejacket, throw on a blanket, and emerge into the corridor. She's concerned by the news, but unflustered – this sort of drama is not new to her. The previous year she'd been serving on *Titanic*'s nearly identical sister ship, RMS *Olympic*, when she was struck and damaged by another vessel.

As a stewardess – and one of only 23 women in *Titanic*'s 900-strong crew – Violet knows it's her job to assist the passengers and ensure their needs are met, no matter what the circumstances, and that is exactly what she intends to do.

 11:50 p.m.

"What's happened, Captain? Why have we stopped?"

Smith, Murdoch and Chief Officer Henry Tingle Wilde (second in command after the Captain) look up from their conversation in the wheelhouse. Before them stands J Bruce Ismay, Chairman and Managing Director of the White Star Line. He's wearing slippers and an overcoat over his pyjamas and looks both worried and irritated.

Behind him, properly dressed in evening wear, is Thomas Andrews, Chief Designer and Managing Director of shipbuilders Harland and Wolff. Ismay might own *Titanic*, but Andrews designed her and oversaw the three-year construction in Belfast. He knows every rivet, bolt and bulkhead, and is taking this first voyage to see how the ship fares and take note of any improvements he can make.

"We've hit an iceberg," Captain Smith says.

Ismay's eyes widen. "Is it serious?"

Smith glances up at a numbered dial on the wall. This is the inclinometer, an instrument that shows if the ship is leaning to one side. Normally, the needle points straight down to zero. However, in the few minutes since the collision, it's crept up to show a five-degree lean to starboard.

"Yes, I'm afraid it is," the Captain replies.

Before Ismay can respond, Fourth Officer Boxhall and John Hutchinson, the ship's carpenter, hurry in. Murdoch doesn't like the look on either of their faces.

"Report, please, Mr Hutchinson," the Captain says.

"I've measured the depth from the fireman's staircase, sir."

"And?"

"The water's already 14 feet deep down there, and rising quickly."

Hichens (who is still standing at the wheel), Wilde, Murdoch, Ismay and Andrews stand in shocked silence.

"All right." Smith draws a hand down his perfectly trimmed white beard. "I want to see how bad things are. Mr Andrews, Mr Wilde – you will accompany me on an inspection. And Mr Murdoch?"

"Yes, sir?"

"Gather all hands and get the lifeboats uncovered. I'll not be caught off guard if things really are amiss."

Down on E-Deck, Violet heads aft, past the ladies' bathrooms and First-Class elevators, then onto the Grand Staircase's lowest landing, where the pristine white of the corridors gives way to soft lighting, warm oak panelling and intricately carved mouldings. The Grand Staircase is the quickest way for First-Class passengers to travel between decks. From here, Violet can see all the way up to the ornate glass-domed roof that covers the Boat Deck landing.

Emerging onto D-Deck, with its plush red carpet, potted palms and green wicker furniture, Violet finds groups of passengers talking about the evening's unusual events. Some had felt the impact. Others slept through it. There's talk of an iceberg. A few are worried about the engines stopping. Most shrug it off and say it's probably just a mechanical issue. Perhaps they've run out of coal, someone jokes. The sense of calm is infectious, and many are already drifting back to their cabins.

On C-Deck, there's a knot of passengers clustered around the enquiries office. The staff behind the desks are advising them, politely but firmly, to return to their beds. It's a similar scene on B-Deck, with passengers dressed in a strange assortment of pyjamas, nightdresses, kimonos, dressing gowns and slippers being assured by stewards that everything is well and the ship will be on its way shortly.

Things are quieter on A-Deck, but Violet notices two men conversing at the bottom of the stairs; the bronze cherub statue poised nearby seems to be listening in on them. Violet knows the man in the coat and pyjamas is Mr J Bruce Ismay, but she doesn't recognise the man in the officer's uniform with the four rank stripes on the cuff.

"How bad is it, Mr Bell?" Ismay says, as she passes.

"It's serious. But I'm hoping the pumps will be able to control the water."

A sudden and terrible din from outside interrupts their conversation. To Violet it sounds like the trumpets of doom.

With her engines stopped, *Titanic* isn't using the steam produced by the boilers. Pressure begins to build until automatic safety valves release and send the excess steam up pipes attached to the black-and-buff coloured funnels. White vapour jets from vents, creating a deafening roar that's audible all over the ship. It sounds like 100 steam trains simultaneously blowing their whistles, and makes normal conversation impossible.

Smith leads Chief Officer Wilde and Thomas Andrews aft down the Boat Deck. All three are worried, and the bellow of venting steam does nothing to soothe their nerves.

"Captain Smith! May I have a word with you?"

It's John Jacob Astor, waving at them from the First-Class entrance leading into the Grand Staircase's topmost landing. Smith draws him inside so they can talk more easily.

"What can I do for you, Colonel Astor?"

"Captain, my wife is not in good health. She has gone to bed, and I don't want to get her up unless it's absolutely necessary. What is the situation? Is it something I should be concerned about?" When Smith hesitates to answer, he adds, "I'm not the panicking kind."

Smith's reply is calm but serious. "You had better get your wife up at once. I fear we may have to take to the boats."

"Thank you, Captain." Astor walks quickly but composedly away.

Smith and his companions descend the Grand Staircase to D-Deck, head along a corridor of First-Class cabins, then down three sets of narrow stairs to G-Deck. They're forward of the bridge now, deep inside the ship and close to where the flooding is. Ahead is a baggage room stacked with trunks and suitcases – all seems dry in there.

To the right stands the doorway that leads into the Post Office Sorting Room. The "RMS" of RMS *Titanic* stands for "Royal Mail Ship", which means she's licensed to carry post between the United Kingdom and the United States. During a voyage, postal clerks work long shifts to sort through 3,364 bags of mail before they arrive in port.

When Smith steps into the sorting room, he sees a sight that would chill the blood of any ship's captain. A harried young postal clerk, drenched to his waist, drags two soaking mailbags across the dark red floor. Shouts and splashes echo up from the stairs leading down to the mail room where the post is kept before it's sorted.

"There's flooding below, sir," the clerk says. "We're trying to save the mail, but it's hopeless."

Whatever emotions Smith feels he hides from his men. "Do your best," he says.

Smith, Wilde and Andrews lean over the railing and peer down into the mail room.

Wilde is less guarded than Smith. "Oh my – " he murmurs.

Two postal clerks, hip deep in swirling water and surrounded by a floating flotsam of letters and parcels, struggle to manhandle mailbags towards the stairs.

"What news, lads?" Andrews calls down.

One of the clerks gestures helplessly around. "As you see, sir."

"We've heard the Cargo Holds are filling up too," the other says. "And the fireman's quarters."

"That's four compartments **breached**," Wilde whispers to Smith.

Andrews crouches at the top of the stairs, sets his stopwatch running and observes as seawater laps below ... around ... and then over one of the steps. "A heavy flood," he remarks. "Let's take a look at the squash court."

Back up the stairs they go and round a corner into the viewing gallery, where a large metal grill overlooks the squash playing area one deck below. A metre of water, transparent green under the bright electric lights, laps gently against the cream-coloured walls; the playing lines beneath waver and dance.

"Do you have what you need to make an assessment, Mr Andrews?" Smith asks.

"I want to check the boiler rooms, then I'll make my calculations."

"Very good. Mr Wilde, let's see how Murdoch's doing with the lifeboats. And we'd better rouse Lightoller and Pitman from their beds, too. I want every officer with me tonight."

11:55 p.m.

"Arms up, my darling. That's it – "

Fourteen-year-old Lucile Carter, who is still sleepy after being woken up, allows her father, Mr William Carter, to lower a lifejacket over her head and tie the straps.

"Do we have to go outside?" she asks. "It'll be cold."

"Your father's just being dramatic," her mother (also called Lucile) says.

"Well, I'm not leaving Billy behind," Lucile's younger brother (also called William) says, and picks up his Airedale Terrier.

"We struck something," Mr Carter says. "I was in the lounge and the ship gave a shudder. One of the stewards said it was an iceberg."

"What of it?" Mrs Carter says. "Even if we did hit something – "

"We *did*," Mr Carter insists. "I felt it."

"Well, it wasn't enough to wake me or the children. And besides, at dinner tonight, Captain Smith himself said he couldn't imagine any condition that would cause this ship to sink. I quote, 'This ship could be cut crosswise in three places and each piece would float'."

"And I have the greatest respect for Captain Smith, but I love my family too much to take such a chance. If something is wrong, I want to be prepared."

"Think of it as an adventure, Mother," Lucile says, and she takes her hand and leaves the comfort of First-Class cabin B96 for the chilly promenades of A-Deck.

Titanic has a crew of around 900. Over half are dedicated to looking after the passengers. Bakers, butchers, fishmongers and chefs feed them. Stewards and stewardesses (like Violet Jessop) answer queries, carry luggage, make beds, serve food and drink, clean cabins, help dress passengers (First Class only) and wash the linen. They are known as the "victualling crew".

Around 300 "engineering crew" are responsible for keeping *Titanic* moving. Greasers keep machinery lubricated. Engineers oversee the engines. Trimmers move coal from huge bunkers into the boiler rooms. Firemen (like Fred Barrett) feed the boilers. Electricians keep the lights, pumps and other equipment running. (*Titanic*'s six electric generators are located aft, behind the engine rooms, and use steam from the boilers to produce power.)

That leaves 66 "deck crew" to carry out routine ship operations. Most are "able seamen", experienced sailors who know how to handle ropes, tie knots and put up a sail. There are also two carpenters (including John Hutchinson) to repair the wooden parts of the ship, six lookouts (including Fleet and Lee) to work in the crow's nest, and the lamp trimmer, Samuel Hemming. Some, such as Quartermaster Hichens, are more senior and work on the bridge, steering the ship and keeping watch. All work directly under the seven officers.

First Officer Murdoch has gathered all the able seamen onto the Boat Deck and ordered them to prepare the lifeboats for launching. He watches as they swarm over the boats, dragging off the canvas covers and releasing their deck moorings. Others stow lanterns and tins of biscuits.

"Do your work as if nothing's amiss," Murdoch shouts over the shrieking vent pipes. He raises a hand as Smith and Wilde approach.

"Get those boats swung out as fast as you can, Mr Murdoch," Smith says. "I've ordered the stewards to gather the passengers on deck with their lifejackets on."

"Are things that serious, sir?"

"I'm afraid they might be. Mr Andrews will have more details shortly, but until then we must prepare for the worst."

Nine-year-old Artur Olsen wakes up when his father, Karl, switches on the light of their Third-Class cabin on G-Deck. It's a small room, only furnished with a sink and bunk beds, but it's clean and tidy, which is good enough for Artur.

The hot running water's a novelty too, and as for the food served in the dining saloon – fresh bread, roast beef, plum pudding! He's never eaten so well in his life.

"Get dressed, Artie," his father says. "I think something's wrong."

As Artur sits up, he becomes aware of a commotion outside: footsteps, raised voices and … splashing? He hops down from the top bunk and gives a cry of alarm as his bare feet land in several centimetres of water.

"Papa?" he says.

Karl hands him trousers, shoes and a jumper. "Put these on. Then your coat and scarf."

Confused, Artur does as he's told while his father packs a suitcase.

"Good boy," Karl says. "Now, take my hand, and don't let go."

More water – enough to cover their shoes – washes in when Karl opens the door. The narrow corridor is full of frightened Third-Class passengers,

many carrying baggage, trying to work their way towards the stairs leading up to F-Deck. Artur grips his father's hand as they push into the crowd.

A steward works his way towards them, handing out lifejackets, banging on cabin doors, and shouting things that Artur, who only speaks Norwegian, doesn't understand. The steward gives Karl his last lifejacket, which Karl immediately puts on Artur. More people emerge from their rooms, adding to the crush.

Rising water swirls around their feet.

15th April, 1912, 12:15 a.m.

"This whole situation is ridiculous," Mrs Lucile Carter says, pulling her coat tighter around her shoulders. "Fancy dragging people out of their beds at this hour."

"They wouldn't be doing it unless they had good reason," Mr Carter snaps back.

"And what is that *terrible* noise?"

"They're letting steam out of the boilers, madam," a passing steward replies. "It's quite routine."

"Well, I wish they would do it more quietly," Mrs Carter says.

The steward gives a well-practised smile. "Please don't worry. This is all just a precaution. We'll be on the move shortly."

The Captain's order to rouse the passengers has reached the ship's stewards and stewardesses, and they're roaming the maze of corridors trying (and often failing) to convince passengers to get dressed and head to the upper decks. Some passengers have joined the Carters outside on the freezing A-Deck promenade, but most remain steadfastly inside, enjoying the warmth and comfortable chairs of the lounge and reading rooms. Unlike Mr Carter, most don't believe there's anything to worry about.

As her parents argue, young Lucile heads aft along the promenade. After ten paces, she frowns and slows down. What a strange sensation … The deck – polished pine and cleared of deckchairs for the night – stretches before her, perfectly level.

And yet it feels to Lucile as if she's walking up a gentle slope. She turns and takes a few experimental steps in the other direction. Yes, it's definitely easier this way, as if she's strolling downhill.

Before Lucile can think any more about this, her mother beckons her over and leads her through the door onto the Grand Staircase landing. "I refuse to turn into an ice cube," she says, making Lucile laugh.

They both turn as a man carrying a bundle of rolled up blueprints under his arm dashes past and takes the stairs to the Boat Deck three at a time.

"I do believe that was Mr Andrews," Mrs Carter says. "Why's he in such a rush?"

"He looked worried," Lucile says.

"He did, didn't he – "

And for the first time, young Lucile detects a trace of uncertainty in her mother's voice.

12:20 a.m.

Thomas Andrews draws Smith, Wilde, Murdoch, Second Officer Charles Lightoller and Bruce Ismay into the navigating room just off the main bridge, leaving the junior officers to carry on preparing the lifeboats.

Andrews unrolls a blueprint showing *Titanic*'s decks and watertight compartments on the glass-topped table. "I've concluded my inspection," he says. "There's heavy flooding in the Peak Tank, Cargo Holds, Mail Room and Number 6 Boiler Room." He turns to the Captain. "That's five consecutive compartments."

"So?" Ismay says.

"*Titanic* can float with four compartments flooded, but not five."

Ismay stares at him. "Are you saying this ship is *sinking*? But she *can't* sink!"

"On the contrary," Andrews replies. "With this amount of damage, she can't float."

"You're mistaken."

"I wish I was. But I designed this vessel, and I know her limits."

"What about the pumps?" Smith says. "We can bail out water from the boiler rooms – "

"That buys us time, nothing more. Look here." Andrews draws a finger along the blueprint. "There's a gash under the waterline around 300 feet long, and even as we speak, the first five compartments are flooding. All that weight's going to drag the bow down."

"What of it?" Ismay says. "The compartments are watertight – "

"Only the floors and walls," Wilde says shakily. "Not the ceilings."

Andrews nods. "Precisely. As the bow sinks, floodwater will climb in the fifth compartment until it spills *over* the watertight bulkhead on E-Deck into the sixth, then the seventh, the eighth ... and so on." He sags into a settee. "This ship will sink. It's a mathematical certainty."

No one speaks. Murdoch recalls the moment he saw the iceberg. Could he have acted sooner? Done something different? Captain Smith stares at the blueprint, trying to think of a solution. Wilde imagines the water pouring into the ship, and rushing down corridors. Lightoller wants to act, to do something, right now. Ismay just shakes his head in disbelief.

"How long do we have?" Smith asks.

"An hour," Andrews replies. "An hour-and-a-half, at most."

"And how many aboard, Mr Murdoch?"

The First Officer's voice catches in his throat. "Two-thousand two-hundred souls."

"With room in the lifeboats for what? Twelve hundred?"

"That's right."

Smith straightens up and faces his stricken officers. "We must abandon ship. The stewards are already gathering the passengers. Mr Wilde, Mr Lightoller, take charge of the port lifeboats.

Mr Murdoch, you take starboard. Get those boats lowered and ready to take on passengers as quickly as you can."

"Yes, sir," they reply.

"Now, listen carefully," Smith continues. "There must be no panic. Keep *Titanic*'s fate to yourselves for now. It's going to be tricky enough evacuating a ship this size at night, even without disorder among the passengers. So, it's up to us to set an example to everyone onboard on how to behave. Understood? Good. To your posts."

The senior officers file out, gathering their wits and glad to have firm orders.

Ismay, white as a sheet, says, "I'll see what I can do to help," and follows them.

Andrews rubs his eyes; to Smith he looks like he's aged a decade.

"A double-bottomed hull, 16 watertight compartments, automatic watertight doors ... I designed this ship to be the safest afloat. No expense spared. She can survive groundings, even a head-on collision with another vessel, but never in a thousand years would I have envisioned her suffering this sort of damage. This whole ghastly situation ... I can hardly bring myself to believe it."

Titanic may be doomed, but the shipping lanes across the Atlantic are busy and the chances are good that another vessel is close enough to come to her aid before she sinks. What's more, she has a loud voice with which to call them.

Directly behind the bridge are the officers' quarters and the wireless radio room. Inside is a desk, chair and a powerful transmitter. It's run by two men, Senior Wireless Operator Jack Phillips and Assistant Wireless Operator Harold Bride, who spend most of their time transmitting and receiving weather reports (including ice warnings) and private messages from passengers: *Having a marvellous voyage. Titanic is a wonder. All my love, Mother.* That sort of thing. Messages are "tapped out" using Morse code – a series of audible "dots" and "dashes" – that the receiver translates into letters, words and sentences.

The wireless had broken down the previous day and it had taken Phillips and Bride hours to fix. Unfortunately, this delay led to a huge backlog of unsent passenger messages, which Phillips – in rather a bad temper – is now wading through. Bride's awake too, getting dressed next door in their shared cabin so he can begin his shift.

Although he knows they've hit something, Phillips is surprised when Captain Smith pokes his head around the door and hands him a slip of paper with the ship's position written on it.

"We've struck an iceberg," he says. "Send the call for assistance."

Now even more surprised, Phillips replies, "Should I use the regulation distress call?"

"Yes, at once."

Phillips and Bride exchange a worried look, then Phillips puts on his headphones and begins to tap out CQD and MGY. CQD was a widely recognised emergency signal, which meant "All stations, distress". Stations meant anyone listening on the line. MGY were *Titanic*'s identifying letters. *CQD … CQD … MGY …* over and over again. The signal travels 1,300 kilometres and is picked up by many ships, including the passenger liner RMS *Carpathia*.

When *Carpathia*'s radio operator replies, a relieved Phillips sends back: *Come at once. We have struck an iceberg. It's a CQD, old man*. Most of the wireless operators working the Atlantic shipping lanes know each other well, so they affectionately call each other "old man" in their message exchanges.

After a shocked pause, the operator taps back: *Should I tell my captain? Do you require assistance?*

Yes, quick.

Help is on its way.

Titanic has eight musicians to provide entertainment throughout the voyage. Led by band leader Wallace Hartley, they consist of three cellists, three violinists, a double bass player and a pianist, and they perform throughout the day in various parts of the ship. Everyone speaks very highly of them.

When the Captain himself asked the band to gather on the Boat Deck to play cheerful music while the passengers evacuate, they did as he asked without question or hesitation.

"Whatever we can do to keep things calm," Mr Hartley says, before putting bow to violin string and leading his band into their first tune.

Assistant Wireless Operator Harold Bride works his way past the crew and officers preparing the lifeboats and enters the bridge.

"Good news, Captain," he says. "The *Carpathia*'s responded and is on her way. She's firing up her boilers and is heading north!"

Feeling a spark of hope, Smith asks, "How far away is she?"

"About 58 miles. Says she'll be with us in four hours."

"And that's the closest ship?"

"Yes, sir."

"Very well. Thank you, Mr Bride. Back to your post, please."

The spark goes out. Four hours. Too long.

Captain Smith now knows with certainty that hundreds of people, likely including himself, won't live to see the morning. He thinks of his wife and young daughter back home in England, who he will never see again.

Then he heads outside to help his men.

12:40 a.m.

Titanic has 20 lifeboats, ten on each side of the Boat Deck. Sixteen are sturdy white wooden rowboats (numbered 1 to 16), which are lowered by hand into the sea from cranes called "davits". The other four lifeboats have wooden floors and canvas sides that have to be pulled up. These "collapsibles" (lettered A to D) can only be launched when the other lifeboats have gone.

Groups of mostly First- and Second-Class passengers, lifejackets on and bundled up against the cold, talk, mill around, and glance uncertainly at the lifeboats.

Second Officer Lightoller cups his hand over Smith's ear and shouts over the still-venting steam: "Shall we begin, sir?"

Smith nods. "Put the women and children in, and lower away."

On the starboard side, Murdoch and Lowe beckon the passengers towards Lifeboat 7, which has been lowered so the **gunwale** is level with *Titanic*'s deck. Ten able seamen stand by the davits, ropes in hand, ready to lower away.

"Ladies and gentlemen," Murdoch says. "The Captain has ordered a precautionary evacuation of the ship, so I'd like to invite the women and children to board the lifeboats first."

"Come forward," Lowe says. "That's it. Gentlemen, please stand back. Thank you."

Herbert Pitman enters the First-Class entrance to the Grand Staircase. "Women and children will kindly proceed to the Boat Deck. Women and children *only*."

But people are reluctant. It's a *long* way down to the sea. Most can't swim, and they're frightened by the prospect of bobbing about in an open boat in the middle of the Atlantic on a freezing cold night.

Why swap the safety of this magnificent ship, which still feels as level and solid beneath their feet as it did in Southampton, with a precarious rowboat?

"We're far safer here than in that little boat," Colonel Astor says, and leads his wife away for the warmth of the gymnasium.

"Please do as the officers say," Ismay implores. "You'll be perfectly safe."

"Oh, very well, I shall go, if I must!" A woman steps forward with her husband, who helps her hop across the gap between ship and gently swaying lifeboat. Inspired by her bravery, a little cascade of women and girls follow. They settle onto the seats, unnerved but making the best of a very strange situation. When the cascade dries up, Murdoch allows a few men to board. Then, with 28 of 65 spaces taken, he shouts, "Lower away!"

Braced against the weight, the seamen begin to let out the ropes. Davits flex, pulleys creak, and in little fits and starts the boat drops down against *Titanic*'s black wall of steel, past **rivets** and brightly lit portholes. Seven long minutes later Lifeboat 7 touches the dark flat ocean without even a ripple.

Quartermaster George Rowe is on duty on the Poop Deck – a raised section at the back of the ship reserved for Third-Class passengers. It's quiet, and there's not much to do except watch the "whiskers around the light" – colourful patterns in the air created by tiny ice crystals floating near the electric lamps.

Rowe noticed the impact and saw the iceberg drift past. To him it felt like a ship coming alongside a dock too heavily. However, he's too far away from the Boat Deck to see what's going on up there, so he's surprised when he notices Lifeboat 7 drifting away from the ship. He telephones the bridge.

"Yes?" comes Boxhall's terse reply.

"Are we carrying out a lifeboat drill?" Rowe asks. "Is that why we've stopped?"

There's a pause as Boxhall realises he's talking to the only crew member who doesn't know about the order to abandon ship. "Come to the bridge," he says. "Bring a box of distress rockets with you."

12:50 a.m.

The moment Lifeboat 7 is safely away, Murdoch and his men move forward to Lifeboat 5. The First Officer is painfully aware that, according to Andrews, the ship has less than 90 minutes before it sinks, and in that short time, he has to get all the lifeboats on this side of the Boat Deck filled, lowered and away from the ship.

As Lowe, Pitman and Ismay cajole passengers to get in, Murdoch does some calculations. Each lifeboat will take at least ten minutes to fill, then around ten more to lower into the sea. So, 20 minutes per lifeboat. That means it will take a minimum of three hours to launch the remaining nine on his side. There aren't enough able seamen to launch more than one at a time. It's too long. *Much* too long.

What's more, the passengers' reluctance to board the lifeboats is hampering their evacuation efforts, and goodness knows how difficult things will become when people realise the ship really *is* sinking. There will be panic, chaos, possibly violence. Not only that, but the officers aren't certain that the davits are strong enough to cope with a full-to-capacity load, and the thought of a lifeboat plummeting into the sea is too awful to think about.

So Murdoch's priority is to lower every lifeboat as soon as he can so they can pick up passengers later from the lower decks, and then from the water after *Titanic* has sunk. It won't do any good if unlaunched lifeboats go down with the ship.

"Mr Murdoch?" It's Violet Jessop. "What can I do to help?"

"You can try and convince this stubborn lot to get in the lifeboat," he says. "And make sure they see your lifejacket. It might convince a few more to put theirs on."

"So, the ship really is in trouble?"

Murdoch lowers his voice. "It is. I advise you to stay up here. I'll make sure you get a place on a lifeboat."

They both look up as the steam exiting the vent pipes slackens and stops, leaving a blissful quiet behind. A few people cheer.

"Well, that makes my job easier," Murdoch smiles.

Once again, Murdoch, Pitman, Lowe, Ismay and Violet begin the frustrating process of encouraging passengers to get into Lifeboat 5. This time, loading is a little easier. *Titanic*'s downward slope is more noticeable and, although the idea of this huge and modern ship actually sinking is beyond most peoples' comprehension, she's clearly been damaged. Pitman and a pair of sailors stand in the dangling lifeboat and help around 34 people inside.

"That's enough," Murdoch says to Pitman. "You take charge of this boat and look after the others when they've launched. Stay close by and when you get a signal try to take more people on from the lower decks."

"Very good," Pitman replies.

Then Murdoch does something that strikes Pitman as rather strange: he puts out his hand (which Pitman shakes) and says, "Goodbye, old man. Good luck to you." To Pitman, this brief exchange feels oddly solemn, almost final, and he can't put his finger on why.

Quartermaster Rowe finds Fourth Officer Boxhall peering out to sea on the starboard wing bridge.

"Take a look out there," Boxhall says. "On the horizon. What do you see?"

"Looks like lights, sir. Is it a ship?"

"I'm not sure. I've been signalling them with the Morse lamp, but I simply can't make out their reply."

"They might not even *be* replying. Could just be stars flickering on the horizon. They're bright tonight."

"Mm."

"I brought the distress rockets."

"Good. The Captain's ordered one to be fired every five minutes."

Passengers gasp and look up as, with a rush of light and a loud hiss, the first distress signal arcs high over the ship and explodes in a shower of blinding white sparks. Lucile Carter thinks it's about the best firework she's ever seen.

"Well, if that really is a ship out there, they're bound to see us now," Rowe observes.

The first six of *Titanic*'s 16 watertight compartments have been flooding since 11:40 p.m. Now, just as Thomas Andrews predicted, her bow is deep enough for water to spill over the top of the watertight bulkhead on E-Deck between compartment six (breached) and into compartment seven (unbreached).

For now, it's just a trickle, barely enough to wet the carpet, but it's getting stronger by the second.

12:55 a.m.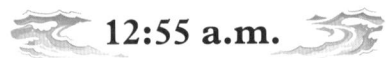

While the struggle to save people is fought on the upper decks, the struggle to keep *Titanic*'s essential systems functioning occurs far below in the boiler, engine and electricity rooms.

Titanic's pumps eject floodwater, buying more time to get passengers off in the lifeboats. Her 10,000 lights allow people to find their way around below decks, and for the evacuation to occur in relative calm – if the lights fail, chaos will follow. And in the wireless radio room, Phillips and Bride continue to signal for help.

All these systems require electricity, and to produce it, the generators need a constant supply of steam from the boilers. At the moment, Boiler Rooms 1 to 4 are dry, so the firemen and trimmers keep them hot so they can feed the generators.

However, Chief Engineer Bell and his men know that if freezing seawater hits pressurised steam – like that in the boilers – it could cause a catastrophic explosion that will turn *Titanic*'s slow descent into an instant one. This is why Leading Fireman Fred Barrett and his men are in the slowly leaking Number 5 Boiler Room, trying to put out the fires in the boilers by hauling the coals out of the red-hot furnaces and into the filthy, yet mercifully lukewarm, seawater swilling around their legs.

"Come on, lads," Barrett cries. "Drag those coals out. That's it!"

Things are relatively calm here. The men work methodically in the swirling smoke and steam, and the steadily chugging pumps are keeping the floodwater under control. However, unknown to them all, floodwater is building up directly over their heads on E-Deck, meaning that despite their heroic efforts to win the battle to save Number 5 Boiler Room, the war to save *Titanic* is already lost.

Suddenly, a cry of agony rises over the sloshing water as Junior Assistant Second Engineer Jonathan Shepherd slips and breaks his leg. Barrett and another engineer called Herbert Harvey help the groaning man into a small pump room, make him as comfortable as they can, then go back to drawing the fires and tending the pumps.

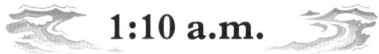 **1:10 a.m.**

The Boat Deck is getting ever-more crowded ... and ever-more sloped.

First-Class passengers are now being joined by more Second- and Third-Class passengers who have managed to navigate their way through the corridors and stairs from their more distant parts of the ship.

Despite growing anxiety and the periodic hiss and flash of the distress signals, there is no panic as the lifeboats are loaded and lowered away. Men say, "Pardon me" and "After you", as they escort their mothers, wives and daughters onto the boats and step away. The cheery music played by Mr Hartley's band lends an air of calm to proceedings and can even be heard on the lifeboats drifting nearby.

Over on the port side, Captain Smith, Wilde and Lightoller are loading Lifeboat 8. An elderly man gently nudges his wife towards them.

"Please get onto the boat and be saved," he says. "Ida, for once in your life, won't you do the selfish thing?"

"No, Isidor." Her tone is adamant. "I shall stay here with you."

Captain Smith recognises the couple as prominent New Yorkers Mr and Mrs Straus and offers both a place on the lifeboat.

"Thank you, Captain," Isidor replies. "But I shall not board that boat while there are still women and children remaining on the ship."

Ida smiles and tightens her grip on her husband's arm. "We have lived together for 40 years. Where you go, I go."

And that was that.

Smith watches the couple link arms and walk away.

Bad news travels fast, and there's none worse than water sloshing around inside a ship.

Passengers and crew located in the forward lower decks have now either experienced or heard about the flooding. Most have a plan: head aft and up, away from the water. Karl and Artur are among them, caught in a crowd that's close to the edge of panic. Stewards shout directions, but their words are mostly lost in the chaos. The narrow, winding corridors all look the same, and there are no signs to follow, or maps to plan a route.

Karl and Artur have struggled up two flights of stairs to E-Deck and now find themselves on the crew alleyway. Nicknamed "Scotland Road", it's a wide service passageway shared by crew and Third-Class passengers that runs nearly the entire length of the ship. Lined with doors and ventilation pipes, it still smells of fresh paint.

They edge forward, carried slowly along with everyone else. They pass sleeping quarters, lavatories, storerooms, and the Engineers' dining saloon, strewn with half-eaten meals as if it's been abandoned in a hurry. Eventually they find a pair of open double doors.

"Through here and up the stairs," a steward cries. "Quick as you can – "

Through the doors they go, into the bottom landing of the Second-Class aft staircase, leading mercifully up. Artur grips his father's hand as they're carried up in the crush. On D-Deck he catches a glimpse of the Second-Class dining saloon, on C-Deck the library, then up to B-Deck where the stairs end. Two doorways lead outside onto the Second-Class promenade.

None of the Third-Class passengers have been in this section of the ship. They're completely lost, and there's no sign of the lifeboats. Where to go? Up? Forward? Back? Karl heads outside then works his way into the Second-Class lounge with its comfortable green chairs and dark wood tables.

"I think it's this way!" someone shouts.

Karl follows the voice and finds yet another set of stairs. However, because so many people have taken a wrong turn, or got lost, or backtracked, or simply given up, there are fewer to slow him down. He hurries up four flights of stairs and eventually exits, exhausted but relieved, through the Second-Class entrance onto the Boat Deck.

Things are still looking good in Number 5 Boiler Room. Not only have the fires been drawn, but the pumps are running ahead of the flooding and the deck plates are actually dry. However, Barrett and his men don't like the groaning sound coming from the forward bulkhead separating them from Number 6 Boiler Room.

"I think we'd better – "

Before Barrett can finish his sentence, the bulkhead collapses, setting loose the thousands of tonnes of water that have been building up behind it. Men, buckets and wheelbarrows are thrown around like so much flotsam. Barrett fights his way to an emergency ladder and heads up. Shepherd, trapped in the pump room with his broken leg, and Harvey, are lost in the deluge.

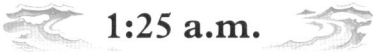

1:25 a.m.

Titanic's bow has dipped low enough for the Atlantic to lap against the portholes just below her nameplate. At the rear, the tips of the propeller blades and a fair portion of her rudder are visible above the water. Her diagonal tilt is clear to the passengers in the launched lifeboats.

But still the lights shine and the music plays.

Towards the stern, a weary Sixth Officer Moody helps Violet Jessop into Lifeboat 16. "Time you were on your way," he says. "Good luck."

The boat is pretty full, and the ropes creak as she hops on board and settles onto a seat. Then Moody cries, "Lower away!" and the boat lurches downwards. Just before it drops below the Boat Deck, Moody reappears and shoves a bundle into Violet's arms. "Here, Miss Jessop, look after this baby."

Knowing nothing about whose child it is, or what mysterious circumstances led to it ending up in her care, Violet holds the infant to her chest and hopes they'll survive the night.

Captain Smith stands on the starboard wing bridge, watching in horror as water trickles, then seeps, then pours over the portside railing into the well deck. Tendrils of green-tinged water spread over the polished pine, picking up the ice chunks left behind by the iceberg.

Bruce Ismay and Thomas Andrews roam the decks and inside areas, trying with increasing desperation to hustle the passengers along.

"Ladies, you must get into the lifeboats!" Andrews implores. "You've no time to pick and choose. Just get in a lifeboat and *go*!"

Fourth Officer Boxhall and Quartermaster Rowe continue to send up distress signals, all the while keeping a hopeful eye on the mysterious lights that might or might not be a nearby ship.

Second Officer Lightoller, drenched in sweat despite the cold, works furiously with his crew. Unlike Murdoch, who's interpreted the Captain's orders as women and children *first*, Lightoller is following a women and children *only* policy and allows no males over 13 into his boats. He even goes so far as to drag out any men who try to take a seat.

"Good evening, madam. Please take my hand and step aboard ... Thank you – "

"Women and children first!" the officer cries over the noise of the crowd. "You there – stay *back*! Women and children *first*!"

Karl crouches in front of a tearful Artur. "I'm going to put you on that lifeboat. But I'm going to have to stay here for a while."

Artur, in a state of shock and frightened by all the confusion and noise, bundles himself into his father's arms. "No, I want to stay with you!"

"I know," Karl says. "But you must do as I say." He grabs a young woman heading for Lifeboat 13. "Excuse me. Could you take care of my boy? His name is Artur, and he doesn't speak English."

"Of course," the woman says.

"Go on now." Karl gives his son a kiss. "It may be a long time before I see you again. Be a good boy, Artie."

Frowning with concentration, Jack Phillips taps out: *We are putting the women and children off in the boats. Cannot last much longer.*

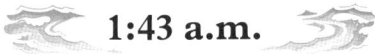
1:43 a.m.

Captain Smith knows his ship is dying.

The bow and forward well deck are completely submerged, which means water is pouring into the cargo hatches, adding more weight and dragging the ship ever-faster towards her doom.

And yet the lights still shine. Their glow is more orange than yellow as the power from the generators slowly fades, but it's enough to see by. Smith gives silent thanks to the brave men down in the electricity room, and hopes they keep the lights burning for a while longer – this unfolding nightmare would be a hundred times worse if it were happening in the dark.

He checks his watch and realises *Titanic* will stay afloat quite a bit longer than Andrew's prediction – long enough, perhaps, to launch all the lifeboats. Small mercies.

The Boat Deck and the A- and B-Deck promenades are now packed with hundreds of passengers: tearful sweethearts embracing, mothers and fathers carrying children, wives refusing to leave their husbands and sons. There's no confusion about their situation now. It's clear to all that the unsinkable ship is sinking, and there are nowhere near enough lifeboats to take everyone. Nearly half have already launched, and there are still around 1,700 souls left aboard.

The previously calm atmosphere is evaporating into one of fear and uncertainty.

Captain Smith is a quietly spoken man, but he can shout when he wants to. "Mr Boxhall, get your sailors to form a line! Don't let those men rush the boats!"

Chief Officer Wilde joins him on the port wing bridge. "It's pretty hairy, sir. Getting harder for us to keep order."

"It's going to get worse." Smith looks out at the drifting lifeboats and puts a megaphone to his mouth. "This is the Captain speaking! Bring those boats back – they're only half filled! Come back in and pick up more people from the lower decks."

But they don't. One lifeboat even rows further away from the ship.

"They're probably afraid of getting overloaded," Wilde says. "Or being sucked down when she goes under."

"Just make sure you fill the rest up before launching," Smith replies.

It takes skill and confidence to handle a lifeboat at sea. Occupants have to be placed in particular positions to maintain balance. Oars and **tiller** need to be handled properly to ensure the boat goes where it's supposed to. One person needs to be in charge, to make decisions and keep everyone in order. All this requires several experienced sailors per lifeboat.

The problem is, *Titanic* doesn't have enough able seamen to properly man every lifeboat and leave enough on the Boat Deck to control the increasingly panicky passengers and handle the ropes and davits. It's yet another complication the officers have to deal with, and one of their solutions is to crew the lifeboats with firemen.

Which is why Leading Fireman Fred Barrett, after evacuating the flooding boiler rooms, finds himself in charge of Lifeboat 13 as it slowly creaks down the side of the ship. He perches at the stern, facing around 70 anxious women and children. Ready with the oars are lookout Reginald Lee and a fireman called George Beauchamp.

"All right, everyone," Barrett calls. "Stay calm and all will be well."

Barrett's not as confident as he sounds. The nearly-full boat is heavy, and he knows the sailors manning the davits are dog-tired. One mistake up there could send them plummeting into the sea.

He peers into a porthole as it jerks past and sees the neatly-made beds and porcelain sink of one of the hospital rooms. Down another deck and there's a Second-Class cabin where two passengers are locked in a tearful embrace. Next deck down is a senior engineer's room. The bed's in a tangle and several drawers are open, as if the occupant woke up and got dressed in a hurry. Then it's just black steel and rivets.

The sea is only around four metres away and is so calm it causes barely a splash against the hull. The ship's ever-steepening angle is shown by the rows of portholes running diagonally down to the waterline, with those submerged casting a sickly green glow. Barrett is shocked when he sees the gleaming starboard propeller almost clear of the water.

Suddenly, directly below, a gush of water pours from an outlet in the ship's side – probably floodwater being pumped from the boiler rooms.

Realising it will swamp the lifeboat, Barrett and some of the passengers shout up to Moody and his men to stop lowering. But they're too far away to hear, and the boat continues towards the torrent.

"Get those oars up!" Barrett yells. "Push us out, for pity's sake!"

Passengers cry in alarm as Fleet and Beauchamp leap up, jam their oars against the hull and try to push the lifeboat away from the gushing outlet. With the passengers' help, they do just enough to prevent the boat being flooded. However, when the lifeboat reaches the sea, the rush of water pushes it underneath Lifeboat 15, which is now being lowered directly on top of them.

Down it comes, a white bulk with a blade-like keel and rounded sides, heavy enough to crush them, break their boat and spill them into the sea. Again, they holler: "Stop lowering! We're right underneath!" But to no avail.

Barrett pulls the lever that's supposed to release the lifeboat from the ropes, but because they're pulled so tight, the mechanism doesn't work: Lifeboat 13 can't move, and Lifeboat 15 is now close enough for him to reach up and touch. As passengers try in vain to push them away, Barrett hacks at the ropes with a knife.

"One, two," he shouts, as the thick ropes fray. "Now – *push*!"

Lifeboat 13 drifts away just as Lifeboat 15 touches down in the spot where they'd been mere seconds before.

The First-Class reception room on D-Deck proved popular with passengers. Beautifully decorated and brightly lit, this open and welcoming space was perfect for family and friends to meet, take tea and relax before dinner.

There's no one here now.

The Atlantic flows from the forward corridors, gulps up from the three elevator shafts and slides over the top step of the Grand Staircase. Its colour perfectly complements the green furniture, stained-glass windows and lush potted palms. Rippling reflections dance on the walls and ceilings.

Mr Hartley's cheerful music drifts down from above. From deep below come creaks, thuds and groans – the doleful percussion of a dying ship.

Jack Phillips hasn't for a moment stopped signalling since Smith gave the order to request assistance. He's exhausted, his head aches, but still he *tap-tap-taps* into the transmitter: *Hurry. Engine room getting flooded.*

 **1:50 a.m.**

The Carter family, instructed by Lightoller to wait until he's ready to load them into Lifeboat 4, huddle on the Boat Deck. Mr Carter's face is grim. Mrs Carter clings to his arm. Their son William carries his dog.

Lucile watches everything with a mix of fear and fascination. The gentle slope she felt at 12:15 has become a steep incline. It was more than strange to think that only two hours ago she was fast asleep in B96 ... and now here she is, in the midst of all this chaos.

A First-Class passenger wearing a tuxedo escorts a woman over. "I'm sure you'll find a place on this one, madam," he says. "Just follow that officer's instructions."

A steward hurries up to him. "Mr Guggenheim, why have you taken off your lifejacket?"

"I've dressed in my best, Etches, and am prepared to go down like a gentleman. If you survive, tell my wife I did my best in doing my duty, and that no woman was left on board because Benjamin Guggenheim was a coward. Tell her my last thoughts will be of her and our girls."

Lucile watches them walk away, looking for more women to help into the remaining boats.

Lightoller addresses the crowd. "Those waiting for Lifeboat 4, follow me. We're going to put you onboard on A-Deck."

The Carters and around 20 others – including Colonel and Mrs Astor – follow him through the First-Class entrance, down the Grand Staircase and onto the A-Deck promenade.

Right back where we started, Lucile thinks.

Lightoller leans out through the window and calls up to his men to lower Lifeboat 4 to them; a glance down tells him the water has crept up to C-Deck. Pouring with sweat, he strips off his greatcoat and starts stacking up folded deckchairs to form makeshift steps up to the windowsill.

"Hello, Lights! Are you warm?" It's Edward Simpson, the ship's Assistant Surgeon, known for his sense of humour.

"Give me a hand with these deckchairs," Lightoller pants.

By the time they finish, the lifeboat's level with the window. Lightoller clambers nimbly through and balances with one foot on *Titanic*'s windowsill and the other on the lifeboat's gunwale.

"All right, ladies," he says, extending a hand. "One at a time, please."

Colonel Astor helps Mrs Astor onto the boat. "May I accompany my wife?" he asks Lightoller. "She's in a delicate condition."

"No, sir," comes the firm reply. "No men are allowed in these boats until the women are loaded first."

Astor nods and kisses his distraught wife's cheek. "The sea is calm, my love. You'll be all right. You're in good hands. I'll meet you in the morning."

Mr Carter does much the same, kissing his family, bidding them farewell and promising to get on another lifeboat. Mrs Carter, Lucile and William sit, utterly bereft, as they watch him retreat into the crowd.

"No dogs – sorry," Lightoller says, and takes Billy from William.

"Don't worry, son," Colonel Astor says. "I'll look after him. I have an Airedale myself."

Assistant Wireless Operator Harold Bride places an overcoat over Phillip's shoulders; Phillips doesn't even look up: *Engine room full up to boilers. Women and children in boats. Cannot last much longer.*

2:00 a.m.

All the main lifeboats are launched, so it's time to prepare Collapsible Lifeboats C and D. These need to be uncovered, that once held Lifeboats 1 and 2, attached to the ropes, then swung out ready to be loaded. It's a complex and exhausting process that Wilde (on the port side) and Murdoch (starboard) oversee in the most difficult circumstances imaginable.

Many passengers have retreated aft as *Titanic*'s bow dips ever-deeper, but many still clamour for a placc on these last remaining lifeboats. Ismay, Andrews and some helpful passengers hurry up and down the Boat Deck shouting, "All women and children, this way!"

Captain Smith watches proceedings from the wing bridges, shouting orders through his megaphone and occasionally glancing behind to see how high the water has climbed.

When there are no more women or children to be seen, Murdoch orders Collapsible Lifeboat C to be lowered, with Quartermaster George Rowe in charge. This is the last lifeboat on the starboard side (apart from Collapsible A, still strapped to the bridge roof). Murdoch says nothing as Bruce Ismay – who has spent the last hour and forty minutes helping other passengers escape – and Mr Carter step into Collapsible C just as it drops below the deck; there is room enough for both of them, but there are also many men left behind who were refused a seat.

Assistant Wireless Operator Harold Bride listens to the screams and chaos coming from outside. All Phillips hears through his headphones are the ever-weakening transmissions from other ships.

We are rushing towards you.

We are lighting up all our boilers as fast as we can.

What is your position, old man?

Captain Smith opens the door. "All right, boys," he says. "You've done your best and can do no more. You'd better take care of yourselves now." Then he's gone.

Phillips turns back to his transmitter and continues to signal. Bride slips a lifejacket over his colleague's head and ties the straps.

Having seen Lifeboat 4 safely away, Lightoller hurries back to the Boat Deck to assist Wilde and his men with Collapsible D. Knowing that there isn't a second to lose, they work in a kind of controlled frenzy, determined to ensure the ship doesn't sink with any lifeboats still attached.

A great scrum of people – mostly male passengers and crew – crowd close as the covers are dragged off. Some panic and throw themselves inside.

With a face like thunder, Lightoller leaps into the boat after them. "Get out, you blasted cowards! Can't you see there are women and children here?"

More afraid of the furious officer than the rising seawater, the men tumble back out of the lifeboat. Realising the situation is getting out of control, Lightoller orders seamen to form a protective line around the collapsible while it's swung out over the side.

Titanic's port-side list is so severe that Wilde thinks the vessel might capsize. When there are no more women and children to load, he orders Lightoller to take command of Collapsible D and leave the ship.

"Not likely," the Second Officer replies. "I'll make room for somebody else." And he clambers up to the bridge roof to see to Collapsible B.

Able to seat over 500 at a time, *Titanic*'s biggest room is the First-Class dining saloon. Passengers were summoned to breakfast, lunch and dinner with a tune from a bugle, and this evening they had enjoyed ten courses, including oysters, salmon, sauté of chicken, roast duck, chocolate eclairs and ice cream.

The tables furthest aft are immaculately set for tomorrow's breakfast: napkins folded into cones, silver cutlery perfectly laid, and printed menus in stands. Delicacies include salmon, haddock, baked apples, sirloin steak, scones, marmalade and honey.

The tables furthest forward are now underwater. Cutlery glitters beneath a surface covered with floating cups and bowls. None of the chairs are bolted down (unusual for an ocean liner), so they drift about, bumping into each other, slowly being lifted towards the ceiling.

Captain Smith puts down his megaphone as water spills over the forward Boat Deck balustrade and creeps towards the bridge. He walks aft with the foaming edge of the Atlantic following at his heels.

"Well done, boys," he says to the remaining seamen. "Do what you can for the women and children, but it's every man for himself now."

Bride shakes Phillip's shoulder and points to the water seeping under the door. "Time to go, old boy."

Phillips drags off his headphones and sighs. "I think the power's gone anyhow. I'm not getting any replies."

By the time they've put on their coats and checked the straps of their lifejackets, the water's risen to their ankles.

"Ready?"

"Ready."

They head out of the wireless radio room, down the corridor and through the door to the Boat Deck. Ropes hang from empty davits. Lightoller and a few others desperately work to get Collapsible B off the roof. Bride heads forward to assist him; Phillips decides aft is the best way to go.

Only a few hours ago, Thomas Andrews had been in his cabin nibbling on a loaf made specially for him by the Chief Baker and making a list of improvements to the ship: a new galley press in the restaurant, alterations to the A-Deck writing room, more screws for the stateroom coat hooks.

Now he stands alone in the First-Class lounge, staring at a painting over the still-smouldering fireplace. The room is at such an obscene angle, he has to lean forward to keep his balance. A glass slides off the mantelpiece and smashes on the floor. A deck of playing cards on a nearby table topples over. Bulkheads groan, panels creak, windows crack in their frames.

This great ship – *his* great ship – is falling apart around him.

Back home in Belfast, probably fast asleep, are his wife Helen and infant daughter, Elizabeth.

He stops the fireplace clock at ten-past-two then heads outside to see what final acts of help he can give.

 **2:10 a.m.**

Lightoller's so engrossed in his work he hasn't noticed that his colleague Hemming, the lamp trimmer, is assisting him. "Hello, Hemming," he says. "Why haven't you gone yet?"

"Oh, there's plenty of time for that, sir," is Hemming's cheerful reply.

With Bride's help, they shove Collapsible B off the roof, but it lands upside down in the swilling water. Murdoch has more luck on the starboard side and manages to get Collapsible A onto the Boat Deck right side up.

These are the last two lifeboats. There are 1,500 people still onboard *Titanic*.

 **2:15 a.m.**

To those on the upper decks, *Titanic*'s slide into oblivion has been slow, almost unnoticeable: the water rises by centimetres; the angle steepens by degrees: so far it's been a stately, dignified demise for a stately, dignified ship. But as the Atlantic pours into cargo hatches, anchor holes, vents and open portholes, swamping the lower decks, rushing up corridors and into cabins, dormitories and staterooms, *Titanic*'s resilience, like her lights, begins to fail …

The great ship gives a sudden forward plunge.

Lightoller nearly falls off the roof. Water tumbles into the bridge. A deep wave rolls up the Boat Deck, washing deckchairs, baggage and people into a black sea that's suddenly ... *right there*.

Passengers further aft see the incoming deluge and flee. The wave gives chase. Some hang onto railings or davits as seawater foams around them. Hemming jumps in and swims as hard as he can towards Lifeboat 4.

Lightoller leaps off the bridge roof. Since going to sea at 13, this tough Lancastrian has sailed the world, been shipwrecked, and prospected for gold in the Canadian wilderness, but none of that's prepared him for the fearsome cold of the North Atlantic. It pierces him like a thousand knives. As the bridge slides into the sea, water pours into a ventilation shaft leading down into the boiler rooms; the inrush is so powerful it sucks Lightoller under the surface and pins him against the grating.

Water wallows higher up the Boat Deck. After catching a glimpse of what might be Captain Smith jumping into the sea, Bride grabs hold of

Collapsible B and somehow ends up inside its upturned hull, gasping in the darkness.

Seeing the mass of terrified people and swirling water rushing towards them, Mr Hartley and his fellow musicians play the final note of their final tune and say their final goodbyes.

Most people swarm towards the stern as the great ship rears out of the ocean, but the steepening decks are smooth, and anything loose – deckchairs, rope coils, lifeboat coverings – slides downward, knocking many over like skittles. Two men shake hands, clamber over the railings and plunge together. Others stand, frozen in terror, as the water closes in.

Lightoller is still trapped by the inrush of water. He is running out of oxygen and bewildered by the deafening *boom* and *crump* of *Titanic*'s destruction. He begins to lose interest in things ... until a blast of warm air rushes up the ventilation shaft and pushes him back to the surface. Grabbing this stroke of luck in both numb hands, he clambers onto Collapsible B's upturned hull ... and finds himself in an utter nightmare of sight and sound.

The sea is full of thrashing, flailing, gasping people. Some sink, others grab floating deckchairs. Some call out for their loved ones. Some try swimming for the ship, others for the collapsible lifeboats. Lightoller leans down and grabs a reaching hand.

Beyond is the impossible, inconceivable sight of the largest ship in existence tipping up like a seesaw.

The bridge and officer's quarters are gone. The angle of her sinking increases at an alarming rate, raising the white **superstructure**, pine decks and black-and-red hull ever-higher into the air.

The five-storey-tall front funnel groans under its own considerable weight. Support cables snap, lashing the water like whips. Metal tears, and the still-smoking funnel topples forward, missing both collapsible lifeboats by centimetres and pushing them away on a foaming wave. Water cascades into the gaping hole left behind, sucking people down into the black depths of the ship.

Anyone on the Grand Staircase is caught in an ambush. Green seawater wallows up from the submerged lower decks, swamping the A-Deck landing with frightening speed. More pours in from the forward corridors, picking up chairs, hurling fixtures, and smashing doors from hinges. Windows shatter under the outside pressure and become frothing whitewater gates, dragging people through from outside.

Then, as this section is pulled beneath the sea, the glass domed roof implodes. Tons of water cascades in, drowning out the cries of those caught in the **maelstrom**. A few manage to get ahead of the water and crawl up the stairs, but far more are swept away.

Titanic's stern rises clear of the sea. Water gushes down the hull. Her lights glow a sullen red. The sound of 47,000 tonnes of ship tearing itself apart is awful. Metal grinds, rivets pop, planks snap; anything not secured falls, crashes and slides.

In Collapsible C, J Bruce Ismay turns away, unable to watch the fate of his ship.

2:18 a.m.

It's a testament to Thomas Andrew's design that *Titanic*'s lights still burn and her hull remains intact, even with her forward sections flooded with 31,000 tonnes of seawater and her aft hovering unsupported in the air. But in the end, the great ship's strength gives out and she splits cleanly in two between the second and third funnels. The noise is deafening. Catastrophic.

Then her lights fail, plunging everything and everyone into darkness.

The bow swings down, splitting decks, exposing *Titanic*'s insides to the sea and dragging the stern section after it until the keel – the vessel's spine – finally snaps.

The entire forward section free-falls into the abyss, leaving a trail of debris behind. The mast snaps back. The second funnel detaches. Entire hull sections peel away. Loose steel cables rip holes in the decks and superstructure.

On the surface, the stern section crashes back onto an even keel, and for a moment of

heart-stopping hope, it seems as if it might stay afloat. But no. The ship is doomed. The third funnel collapses like a felled tree. Water surges into the exposed corridors, rooms and stairwells and – along with the weight of her three massive engines – drags the stern section down until her rudder, propellers and elegant clipper-style stern are pointed directly up at the cold, indifferent stars.

# 2:20 a.m.

Chief Baker Charles Joughin was in charge of producing the thousands of loaves, buns, biscuits, pastries and pies that were consumed daily by passengers and crew. He was asleep in his cabin on E-Deck when the iceberg was struck. As soon as he heard that the lifeboats were being prepared, he ordered his staff of bakers to provision them with bread. He then helped passengers escape, refused to leave when offered a place in Lifeboat 10 and threw 50 deckchairs overboard to act as floats.

He's below deck when *Titanic* breaks in half, yet somehow, amongst all the destruction, noise and panic, manages to end up at the back of the ship. He crouches on the safety rail just above *Titanic*'s nameplate, and stares down the vertical deck at the sea 50 metres below.

Joughin is not alone. Hundreds more people – crew and passengers of all classes and ages – cling to davits, winches and cranes, and huddle on deckhouse walls and sections of superstructure that have now become floors. Besides the groans of the stricken ship, the air rings with shouts of disbelief, declarations of love, and cries of terror.

For those who keep their grip the agonising wait for the ship to drop beneath them is accompanied by the rolling thunder of boilers, bulkheads, furniture and fittings succumbing to gravity inside.

Then comes the final plunge. *Titanic* angles to port as her descent into the frothing water quickens. As the sea rushes up inside the remains of the ship, any pockets of air left burst out of windows and portholes with the wet hissing sound of a hundred spouting whales.

Joughin is the last person to leave, swimming away as the stern slips beneath the waves with little more than a gulp.

He doesn't even get his hair wet.

It's been two hours and 40 minutes since the collision.

It's pitch black. *Titanic* is gone. Twenty lifeboats (one upside down) drift around the wreck site. A smoky vapour hangs in the freezing air. The Atlantic's temperature is an unsurvivable two degrees Celsius below zero. The closest land is still 640 kilometres away; the seabed four kilometres down.

There are around 1,500 people in the water. None of the lifeboats return for them. Some people argue hard to do so, but they're outnumbered by those afraid of being capsized or swamped. Besides, many lifeboats have rowed too far away to be of any use. Instead, the shivering survivors sit, and wait, and endure.

Finally, after an eternal hour, the sound of those in the water fades to a silence broken only by the creak of nearby icebergs.

Epilogue

When the cries of those in the water subsided, Fifth Officer Harold Lowe deemed it safe to look for survivors. He picked up four, one of whom later died. The rest, around 1,514 people, perished.

At 4.00 a.m., after steaming as fast as she could through the ice field, RMS *Carpathia* arrived, picked up around 710 survivors and took them to New York.

Titanic's fate sent shockwaves around the world. Two enquiries were set up to find out what had happened. Within days, many of the deeply traumatised survivors had to relive their experiences while giving evidence. Public interest in the event was enormous, and in 1912 no fewer than three films were made about the disaster, including one starring actress Dorothy Gibson, who was a passenger on the ship.

The tragedy brought about important changes. From then on, ships had to carry adequate lifeboats, crews had to carry out regular lifeboat drills, and radios had to be operated 24 hours a day.

An organisation called the International Ice Patrol was set up to monitor icebergs in the North Atlantic. It still operates today.

It's impossible to measure the sheer scale of loss and trauma caused by *Titanic*'s sinking. There are the many who died, and the family and friends left behind to mourn. Survivors paid a toll too, haunted for the rest of their lives by the memory of that terrible night.

Lookout Frederick Fleet survived and ended up working on RMS *Olympic*.

Reginald Lee survived but died of heart failure a year later.

First Officer William Murdoch didn't survive.

After giving his place on Lifeboat 14 to Fifth Officer Harold Lowe (who survived), Sixth Officer James Moody went down with the ship.

Chief Engineer Joseph Bell and his engineers, electricians and plumbers worked until the very end to pump floodwater and keep the lights and radio functioning. He, along with his men, perished.

Quartermaster Robert Hichens survived.

John Jacob Astor perished; Madeleine Astor and her unborn child survived.

Lamp trimmer Samuel Hemming made it to Lifeboat 4 and survived.

Leading Fireman Frederick Barrett survived and went on to work on RMS *Olympic*.

Fourth Officer Joseph Boxhall survived and spent the rest of his career at sea, including as Second Officer on RMS *Olympic*.

Thomas Andrews went down in the ship he had lovingly designed and built.

Violet Jessop survived.

Chief Officer Henry Tingle Wilde went down with the ship, as did Carpenter John Hutchinson.

Joseph Bruce Ismay survived, as did the whole Carter family.

Second Officer Charles Lightoller and Assistant Wireless Operator Harold Bride survived on the upturned Collapsible B. Third Officer Herbert Pitman also survived.

Artur Olsen survived. His father, Karl, did not.

Senior Wireless Operator Jack Phillips perished.

Wallace Hartley and his musicians went down with the ship.

Quartermaster George Rowe survived.

Isidor and Ida Straus died, presumably together.

Benjamin Guggenheim went down with the ship, dressed in his finest. His steward, Henry Etches, survived.

Assistant Surgeon Edward Simpson died. Chief Baker Charles Joughin survived, despite being in the water for several hours.

Captain Edward Smith went down with his ship.

Glossary

breached broken through, opened

dampers devices that reduce the amount of oxygen feeding a fire

engine telegraph device used to transmit orders from the bridge to different areas of a ship

gunwale the upper edge of the side of a ship or boat

maelstrom violent turmoil, chaos, destruction

maiden voyage the first trip of a newly built vessel

reciprocating steam engines powerful steam engines that use one or more pistons to power the propellers

rivet a metal bolt used to hold metal plates together (*Titanic* had around three million rivets)

spur a pointed piece of ice

stewards male crew members whose job was to look after the passengers

stewardess female crew members whose job was to look after the passengers

superstructure the parts of a ship that are above the main deck

tiller a lever used to steer a boat or ship

Book talk questions

What does the story of *Titanic* teach us about courage and sacrifice?

Can you think of a difficult time when you had to be brave?

What lessons can we learn from the *Titanic* disaster that are still relevant today?

How did the passengers and crew show friendship and support to each other during the crisis?

How do you think the passengers felt as the ship was sinking?

Why do you think the story of *Titanic* continues to capture people's interest today?

Why is it important to listen to the stories of the survivors?

Did any people in the book particularly interest you? Why?

Do you think something could have been done differently in that situation?

Many passengers were travelling to start new lives. What dreams do you think they had?

Ask the author

What kind of research did you do to write this book?

Lots of reading. *A Night to Remember* by Walter Lord and *On a Sea of Glass* by Tad Fitch, J. Kent Layton and Bill Wormstedt are both brilliant books. There are lots of great *Titanic* documentaries and websites too.

Matt Ralphs

What was the main theme you wanted to convey in your book?

Courage. There are many examples that we know of where people showed courage in the direst of circumstances, and no doubt countless more that were not remembered or reported.

Which particular story or aspect of *Titanic* captivates you the most?

So many to choose from! The size, beauty and ingeniousness of the ship's design, from her dazzlingly luxurious staterooms, sweltering boiler rooms, and the less well-known hidden nooks and crannies.

What was the most challenging part to write?
The ending. The last moments of the ship and the 1,500 souls who went into that deadly water. Conjuring such a dreadful scene in my mind, holding it there, then putting it into words – that was difficult.

What other resources would you recommend to someone who wants to learn more about *Titanic*?
A creator called Oceanliner Designs makes lots of fascinating *Titanic*-related videos. Also, Titanic Honor and Glory have created an explorable virtual recreation of the ship. It's a true work of art. Both were invaluable in my research.

What was your favourite book as a child?
I read *A Night to Remember* by Walter Lord when I was young, which must have planted a seed in my mind that led me to writing this book.

If you could meet any historical figure from *Titanic*, who would it be?
Mr Thomas Andrews, so I could ask him lots of questions about his incredible ship.

Published by Collins
An imprint of HarperCollins*Publishers*

The News Building
1 London Bridge Street
London SE1 9GF
UK

Macken House
39/40 Mayor Street Upper
Dublin 1
D01 C9W8
Ireland

Text © Matt Ralphs 2026
Design and illustrations © HarperCollins*Publishers* Limited 2026

Matt Ralphs asserts his moral right to be identified as the author of this work.

10 9 8 7 6 5 4 3 2 1

ISBN 978-0-00-878472-0

All rights reserved. No part of this publication may be reproduced, stored in a retrieval system, or transmitted in any form by any means, electronic, mechanical, photocopying, recording or otherwise, without the prior written permission of the Publisher or a licence permitting restricted copying in the United Kingdom issued by the Copyright Licensing Agency Ltd, 5th Floor, Shackleton House, 4 Battle Bridge Lane, London SE1 2HX.

Without limiting the exclusive rights of any author, contributor or the publisher of this publication, any unauthorised use of this publication to train generative artificial intelligence (AI) technologies is expressly prohibited. HarperCollins also exercise their rights under Article 4(3) of the Digital Single Market Directive 2019/790 and expressly reserve this publication from the text and data mining exception.

British Library Cataloguing-in-Publication Data
A catalogue record for this publication is available from the British Library.

Author: Matt Ralphs
Illustrator: Elena Dall'Aglio (Advocate Art)
Publisher: Laura White
Commissioning editor: Holly Woolnough
Development editor: Zoë Clarke
Product manager: Holly Woolnough
Content editor: Selin Akca
Copyeditor: Sally Byford

Proofreader: Catherine Dakin
Reviewer: Lisa Davis
Fact checker: Sasha Morton
Cover designer: Sarah Finan
Internal designer: 2Hoots Publishing Services Ltd
Typesetter: David Jimenez
Production controller: Sophie Waeland

Collins would like to thank the teachers and children at Grange Primary School, Southwark, for being part of the development of Big Cat Read On.

Printed in the UK

MIX
Paper | Supporting responsible forestry
FSC® C006032

Made with responsibly sourced paper and vegetable ink

Scan to see how we are reducing our environmental impact.

Get the latest Collins Big Cat news at
collins.co.uk/collinsbigcat